LOYALTIES CURSE

Poetry Book Vol. 1

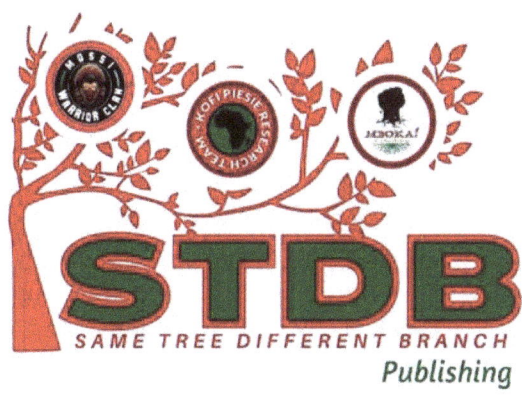

© Kofi Piesie Research Team Same Tree Different Branch

Kofi Piesie

Copyright 2024 by SameTree Different Branch Publishing

All rights reserved. No Part of this book may be reproduced or transmitted in any form or by any means, electronic or mechanical, including photocopying, recordings, or by any information storage and retrieval systems without the written permission of the publisher.

Printed in the United States of America

ISBN 979-8-9896372-3-2

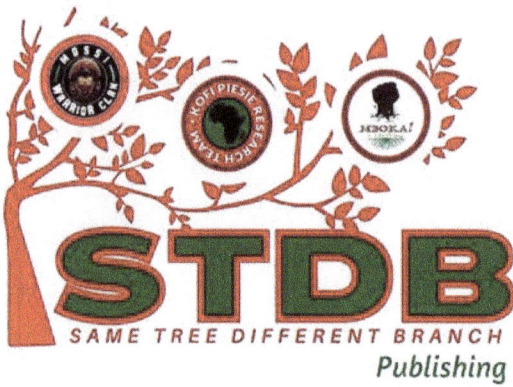

About The Author

My Name is Pierre Joseph. I was born in the Bronx, NY, and raised in Far Rockaway Queens and Philadelphia. I'm 43 years of Age a Father of 2 Nakeem (26) And Samya (14). I began Writing at the age of 11 after a Traumatizing experience that took place at the age of 9. I was shot multiple times after a robbery gone wrong. This experience made me very timid as a Child. I didn't like to argue or fight with anyone because I believed that any violence would lead to me being shot again, and that terrified my Soul for many Years. With all these feelings bottled up, I began to write about many things that haunted me. Writing became my therapy, my personal release from all things I couldn't understand Sadly, when I was 18, my Mother was Diagnosed with Cancer, 2 years later, she Passed away. This Event had me in Rage and Full of Anger. I began to Rebel in the Worst way, and I made plenty of Mistakes. I began to write again as a way to release my Inner Demons. I try to balance my work, but some of it goes into a Dark area, but that has been My life: a Mixture of Sunshine and Rain.

Loyalties Curse
POEM ONE

Poem One

They didn't put you to bed, but they left your Body sleeping, the score is 100-3, There's no way to get even, Thought you would be around, didn't know you was leaving, Made the call on a Friday, you didn't make it through the Weekend, Rocking back and Forth, now your momma is Grieving, She at a Loss for words, so she still ain't speaking, didn't See a Thing, she don't know who she Seeking, Reverend was Busy, so she had to call the Deacon, Strength in your Soul, but your Body is Weakend, Started with a Small hole, he didn't know he was leaking, Told him to hold his breath, and he still ain't breathing, Pushed him to the Back, so he still ain't Leading, It didn't just Happen it Happened for a Reason, Caught with Salt and Pepper, he didn't have the Right Season, There was no juice left, but still he squeezing, Alergic to the Game, but he ain't sneezing, Smile for the Camera, You know he Cheeseing, Made you a Dinner Plate, Now we Eating.

Loyalties Curse
POEM TWO

Poem Two

I was Born to Grow, don't be late,730 I'm starting the Show, yea it's all gone, but you move it to Slow, Cold World it's 40 below, you didn't tell me everything, how much more do you know, Don't Overstay your Welcome, it's time for you to Go, all out of thread, how much did you sew, a loaf of bread, I did it for the dough, I seen 5 Catch, how many did you throw, Stand Tall, it's time to get Low, Set me on Fire, I only got one Chance to Blow, Get on the Good Foot, But I hurt my Toe, Run with the River, It's all about the Flow,10 feet Deep, I'm buried in Snow, Can't play both sides, Cobra Commander Or G.I.Joe, Beat up your Face, But there's No K.O Took too many Loses, that's 5 in a Row, LIFE is Too Short, I still need Time to Grow.

Loyalties Curse
POEM THREE

Part Three

If you go to War, you better win, most of your enemies use to be a friend, didn't come by myself, but Probably in the end, spin a couple blocks, who gon bend, the line between Love and Hate, is Pretty Thin, didn't get caught the first time, so we did it again, it's all about the family, whose your next of Kin, Looking for Myself, I was Lost from Within, Couldn't be Like You, Comfortable in my Own Skin, My Hearts been Traumatized, I ain't the Same from back Then, Strong as I Need to Be, I can take it on the Chin, I promise to Make it Back, Loyalty is my Only Sin.

Loyalties Curse

POEM FOUR

Poem Four

The Top is only for those that climb, Get yours, I'mma get mines, Pay attention to the message in the middle, read between the Lines, The World has a Proper meaning, explore what it defines, Be Patient with the Labels, Read all the Signs, Be careful with the Change, I'm talking Nickles and Dimes, Success comes after Failure, Thats the Brillance of Your Mind, Search Within Yourself, And Greatness you Will Find, Handle Pressure like a Diamond, and even in Darkness You Will Shine, He made the Impossible, Possible, And turned My Water into Wine.

Loyalties Curse
POEM FIVE

Poem Five

I Will dig you up just to give you a new Grave, put away the surfboard. I'm riding a new wave, out here splurging; how much did you save, in God we trust, how much do you praise, nothing Old under the Sun, Now crime got new ways, gotta save the seeds, be proud who you raised, gotta be patient, a little time between days, Already gone but watch for who Stays, bullets have no name, so watch for loose Strays, facial recognition, We enter a new Phase, can't understand, that's wicked in new ways, Anything you ask, just give me a few Days, Stack your chips up, divide them a few ways, Who you looking for, I'm the Trouble that you Crave, What you looking for, First Puzzle a New Maze, limited options, A couple of Numbers and a Few Ks, Watch the Business for who Pays, Old thoughts for New Days.

Loyalties Curse
POEM SIX

Poem Six

When all my Dreams came true, My Perception of Darkness gave me a Birds Eye View, My Hunger for Understanding gave me something I couldn't chew, standing in front of Tomorrow, what am I supposed to Do, I know I need more, but there's only Room for a few, behind the 8 ball, I'm right on que, walk on the edge of Midnight, It gotta be the Shoe, Exploring the Earth, talking about what I ain't gon do, Men of Respect, a Lesson Learned from a Few, My word and my Balls, I only have the 2, you can't put me together, if you missing a Screw, Surrounded by Who I Trust, There's no me Without You.

Loyalties Curse

POEM SEVEN

Poem Seven

Everything can't be All Right, if you got Nothing left, apologies from a Grown Man, some things you gotta Accept, Stand in Front of A Bullet, what are you willing to Protect, I got a couple options, so I'm willing to Select, a different kind of view, You ain't seen nothing yet, brand new roommate, got you living with regret, don't want to think about it, now you got something to forget, Put you in the Back, You something to Neglect, kill all the germs, when you use disinfect, Heavy is the Head, you gotta protect your Neck, handing out the Truth, don't take it as a Threat, One way road, only leads to Disrespect, still working with the Lord, He ain't through with me Yet, Treated like a Dog, you got Views from a Pet, Everything is all Wrong, you got a Choice to Correct.

Loyalties Curse

POEM EIGHT

Poem Eight

If I don't know where I'm going, how can I give you Direction, looking for the Better part of Myself, I'm Searching for Perfection, Comfortable in the Arms of Strength, I need your protection, sometimes you gotta choose, make your Selection, Power of the Skin, there's no privilege in your complexion, protected by 2 men, call them Smith and Wesson, die behind my word, there will be no confession, Never Seen me Before, what was your first Impression, Under 17, View at your own Discretion, Band-Aid Understanding, Every Scar came with a Lesson, Never in a million years, there's no recollection, Negative and Positive, there's no Connection, Lust without trust, there's no affection, I'm just happy to be here, Every Breath is a Blessing.

Loyalties Curse
POEM NINE

Poem Nine

Even if you Cut out his Tongue, He still Gunna Tell, Everybody don't deserve Heaven, Some deserve Hell, Turtleneck Skid mark, beat you out your Shell, Never trip over Blocks, if I never Fell, Can't keep the truth from a Blind Man, Tell the truth in Braille, Leave you on a Cross, Hammer every Nail, Old food from a Arab, The Chips are always stale, Colorful arrangements, Black Blue and Pale, The Weight on my Shoulders, I need another Scale, Give it all I got, With no plans to Fail, Crowed at the Top, but it's Lonely in this Cell, No one heard you Scream, They will never hear you Yell, No direction for Freedom Until I'm out of Jail, They called me a Flight Risk, I didn't make Bail, Uncomfortable Position, Let's see if he Tell.

Loyalties Curse

POEM TEN

Poem Ten

One way in, No way out, Swim with the Sharks, But can you Survive in a Drought, Didn't understand the Lesson, But you know what it's about, Good deeds done in Silence, No need for the Clout, This Road goes Nowhere, Time to pick a new route, If no one can hear you Scream, what's the use in a Shout, Stand on Every Word Given, Leave them with No doubt, Promise to walk you Down, That's the honor in a Scout, Pitch these balls Long term, Without Striking Out, Never say a Thing, Words taste like Guinness Stout, Gone to November, Them birds fly south, Chess pieces and puzzles, You gotta figure them out, Everybody knows what they're doing, Until they get punched in the Mouth, Evil waits at your Front Door, But there's no getting inside the House.

Loyalties Curse

POEM ELEVEN

Poem Eleven

Skeptical about Loyalty without Reason, Prepared for any Storm, Dress Right for the Season, Wolf in Sheep's Clothing, your Really a Demon, Can't trust a Soul, Too many out here Scheming, Can't Believe this World, I really think I'm Dreaming, Lucky to Be Alive, I don't know how you Breathing, Last time I saw you, You was out here Screaming, Blood on the Dance Floor, Got you out here Cleaning, Can't catch your Breath, So you out here Weezing, Wicked in the Flesh, Now you out here Grieving, You won't See Tomorrow, This will be Your Last Evening, Beef is Well cooked, All it needed was the Seasoning. I Did it for Nothing, That's Rhyme without Reasoning.

Loyalties Curse

POEM TWELVE

Poem Twelve

Let me live amongst the Stars, no better place to meet her, can't touch your body and Soul without a Feature, Mouthwatering taste of Despair, Can you keep Her, Scorch the Earth, and Kiss the Son, But can you go Deeper, Get back what you gave, The time of the Reaper, Didn't hear me when I walked in, Admire the Sneaker, What don't kill you won't make you Strong, Your presence gets weaker, No direction across the street, Left or Right Blinker, Cold lessons from the Old Man, Made me a Thinker, Can't hear you when you Scream, It might be the Speaker, Six feet deep, you can find me Beneath her, Gone for 7 days, I might have to Week her, With Love and Affection, I plan to Greet Her, Only one Problem I still gotta Meet Her, Destiny awaits for those that Seek Her, Something that I want, But I will never need her. King of Oneself, you know the Procedure.

Loyalties Curse

POEM
THIRTEEN

Poem Thirteen

Deeper than empty pockets, gone fast like 2 Rockets, talked about, New topics, feel the breeze, summer tropics, down bad, no profits, 4 walls, no closets, withdraw, no deposits, Demon Time, no Prophets, stomach hurts, he vomits, couple of likes, no comments, Orange juice, and 2 omelets, my word, you promised, No Lie, you Honest, get even, with the oddest, Vanilla and Hot Chocolates, gone up, New stock tips, No Worries I got This, New brooms and Mop Sticks, Food for Chopsticks, believe your Optics, No Brakes, Can't stop This.

Loyalties Curse

POEM FOURTEEN

Poem Fourteen

America's Nightmare, I'm what you see when you realize what you put here, understandable mistreatment provoked by your Fear, Skin made Jackets, gave you something to wear, adolescent black child, with fruits to bare, Strength in your DNA, we got Roots to Share, The Truth is Rare, the Youth Prepare, like you was there, no here nor there, Don't Move or stare, to smoove be Clear, The Wolf Beware, I use to Care If you was here, I use to wear, a newer pair, a few will spare, It Boom and Glare, Dog Walk, you got Human Hair, The Truth Will Dare, Use your Pair, The Proof Is Here, You Rule through Fear, who you scare, 20 20 you be clear, No Balance, You be fair. Sit down and use your Chair.

Loyalties Curse
POEM FIFTEEN

Poem Fifteen

Here to Face the World, but Pardon my Back, wasn't Born with it, its something you Lack, Prey on the Enemy, Be Slow to Attack, Make them feel comfortable, that's how you Attract, rock that baby to sleep, supply every Snack, if this is done Correctly, they have no time To React, 100s,50s, and 20s, divide every stack, Make sure the Gift from God, ain't all that you Pack, The Vision between the Door, Small like a Crack, Love From a King, that's Golden and Black, Problem with Your Computer, it's probably a Hack, Kill for a Lie, Die for a Fact, Neck Turned Sideways, You Probably Snapped.

Loyalties Curse
POEM SIXTEEN

Poem Sixteen

It's Never about what you offer, only about what you give or what you brought her; standing in Shadows, don't make you a Stalker, discipline from a backhand, why I aught ah, sizzling piece of bacon, that pigs for the slaughter, no safety net, damn Right I caught her, ice around your neck, Fresh cup of frozen water, life or death Choice, I gotta feed my daughter, for this book of life, I am the author, it didn't kill me, So it made me stronger, Right to remain Silent, where is my Lawyer, Just Us Get Served, Four Pound Sig Sauer, Waste of a Brilliant Mind, What have you Taught Her, No Receipt for what you Buy, Where have you Bought Her, Lifes a Beach, But there's Sharks in the Water.

Loyalties Curse

POEM SEVENTEEN

Poem Seventeen

A Lion is a Lion in Every Jungle; Fall short, Run Fast, Don't Stumble, don't forget the best parts of the struggle, practice, and preparation, diamond formation in the huddle, prepare for the rain, sunshine and the puddle, Nowhere To Go, I got no place to run to, spin the block quick and easy as 1,2, fighting for your life, Rumble Young Man Rumble, dropped on the floor, now watch your cookie crumble, forgot about the knife, But you know what the gun do, art of war, Paint a Picture like Sun Tzu, smile on my face, like my Son Do, Don't forget I had fun too, look how far, we have come to, Can't Feel when I Touch You, No way to be Subtle, Walk down who you run through, I ain't looking for Trouble, Gorillas make Monkeys Humble, Iron or Concrete, we Still in the Jungle.

Loyalties Curse

POEM
EIGHTEEN

Poem Eighteen

Born a mannequin, your mother raised a dummy, gave you everything I got, you can never take nothing from me, over my dead body, There's no man above me, other than my daughter, nobody loves me, seek my own justice, no man can ever judge me, Can't hug the Block, I'm not there emotionally, keep it to yourself, Think when you approaching me, Can't go 50/50 I'm all in Totally, behind closed doors, We do this Openly, No Mixed Words, Say it Right if you Quoting Me, Brand New High, With a Different kind of Potency, everything allegedly, All done Supposedly, Dark Shadows, Never notice me, Never say a Word, You won't hear me Vocally, Tomorrow ain't Promised, I'll see you There Hopefully.

Loyalties Curse

POEM NINETEEN

Poem Nineteen

Like Seeds in the Field, you gotta watch me Grow, be patient with the Process, even if it's Slow; communication is the main part, so you gotta let me know, never hold me back, you gotta let me Go, Mix flour and water, I'm trying to make a little dough, calm as the River, you gotta let it flow, catch me on front line, face to face, Toe to Toe, Don't know all the Characters, But you the Star of the Show, if you don't know anything, it's one thing you should Know, When you Stand next to the Light, Even In Darkness you can Glow, Lost at a Stop Sign, No green light will let you Go, Cane Killed Abel, I can't even Trust My Bro, Walk this Earth like a Stranger, Nobody cares who you know, How Well Kept is Your Harvest, You reap what you Sow.

Loyalties Curse

POEM TWENTY

Poem Twenty

How do you kill what's already dead, spin the block 3 times, the introduction to lead,4 to the body,3 to the head, 2 to the back, put 5 in your leg; you'll never be able to stand on any word that you said, outlined in chalk, memories under your bed, bit off more than you can chew, same hand that made sure you got fed, never say a thing, odd numbers getting Pled, it's all down Hill better go and get your Sled, I can see your true colors, white meat and blue blood that turns Red, always another way, you could have did it instead, tried to share my loaf, now give me back my Bread, Died on the Block, deceived by Street Cred.

Loyalties Curse
POEM TWENTY-ONE

Poem Twenty-One

The Reality of Confidence, a complete lost of Trust, last of a dying breed, there's no more of Us; Deception changed your Pockets, no longer a useful Crutch, I called you my Brother, Cain separated the line between Us, Focused on your Demons, you became more of the Same, Destiny's Backdrop, your the only one Left to Blame, Blindfolded cant apologize, You Pointed your Finger at a Picture in a Frame, Call him your Leader, who you follow in Shame, Blue Collar White Shirt, you became the worst kind of Stain, Elevation from a Nightmare, Wrong Turn, we going insane, Disrespectful Violence, Like Taking your Grandmama Chain.

Loyalties Curse

POEM
TWENTY-TWO

Poem Twenty-Two

You think your the Only You that exists, can't apologize for your decisions, enter at your own Risk, Unlawful Nightmare, like when they stop and Frisk, pay attention to your target, if you aim, don't Miss, introduction to the Ocean, where you learn to Fish, Genie in a Bottle, here to grant a Wish, yesterday it was two tings of sardines and a Bread, but today where Rich, Eat the food of a working man, but promise to Never Snitch, T.V. on the Same Channel, my loyalty will never Switch, if you scratch, I scratch, I'm here to relieve a itch, a Different kind of Fabric, it's gonna be hard to Stitch, Surround yourself with Dog Food, Your gonna end up like Mitch.

Loyalties Curse

POEM TWENTY-THREE

Poem Twenty-Three

Things just ain't the Same, for what remains, so many holes, so many stains, assaulted a beautiful mind, he lost half his brains, the evil that men do, responsible for the fire in my Veins, unfortunate lose lose,2 quarters, symbolize change, death was in arms reach, the smell in the air, seems kind of strange, couldn't recognize your Beauty, your face got rearranged, Heart did a Slow dance, stop Beating from words that were exchanged, promised to Stay yourself, but the Lost of Life Provides a Strain, never known this before, this is your introduction to Pain, No safety net when you fall, can't provide a Crutch or a Cain, Metro Card or Token, you still gotta Take the Train, Same road with a different destination, I had to make my own lane, Survive a world meant For Cats and Birds. Real-life Tiger vs. Crane, call me anything you want but never provide my name. Search for the Root in Forgiveness; you have nothing left to Claim. Tuesdays may Look alike, But no 2 days are the Same. Stand Next to the Bulls Eye. I'm trying to Find my Aim; nobody cares where you Going; til you Forget about where you Came.

Loyalties Curse

POEM
TWENTY-FOUR

Poem Twenty-Four

He Said a Goat to a God, is nothing but a Sacrifice; Head Up, Eyes Open, is my Best Advice, Humble yourself when you Speak; I won't ask you Twice; we can negotiate the Cost, that's just my asking Price, You Gamble with your life, so you pass me Dice, Frozen Food wrapped in Sheets, that's just my Bag of Ice, Kill you and your Father, Make Them a Bastard twice, It's a cost to be the Boss, and you paid the Price, Put you on a Plate, next to the red beans and Rice, If I paid full price, I don't want Half my slice, middle man Taxes, I tweaked the Price, no attitude Given, You must be nice, Kill all Rats Involved, why you run from Mice, You might Die for my Involvement, Whats your Sacrifice.

Loyalties Curse

POEM TWENTY-FIVE

Poem Twenty-Five

With no real direction, I can't find my way home, with no recollection, I can't remember the things I've been shown, Go Against the Government, you'll Probably End up a Clone, I already know where you've been, just let me see your phone, Never Change the Skin I'm In, I'm Loyal to The Bone, Uncomfortable in a Chair, Heavy is the Head that Sits on the Thrown, Privately ill Pop Your Top, Go get your Brain Sewn, Never Had a Chance to Be a Child, These Booster Shots will stop you from getting Grown, Surrounded by Who I Can Trust, You'll probably Catch me All Alone, Sharks can usually smell Fear, I wear a different kind of Cologne, Powerful Rock Formations, all Set in Stone, Front Page Headliner, Wrong way to get your Name Known.

Loyalties Curse

POEM
TWENTY-SIX

Poem Twenty-Six

Blood on the Cotton, Razor on the Wire, Last Day of Work, New Chance to Hire, Flammable Liquids, might set your Ass on Fire, Telling the Truth when you Scared, made me a Liar, Highway to Hell, you might need a Tire, True words from God, that we sing to the Choir, Born on the Top Floor, no way to get Higher, King of Ones Self, Now control your Desire, Secret Society, One thing we Require, This Product Sells itself, All we need is a Buyer, You might Wet yourself, All you need is a Dryer, I've been Working all My Life, No Plans to Retire, Angels with Broken Wings, No way to get Flyer, Too many Screws Loose, Pass me a Plier, Promise to Walk you Down, Til the day you Expire.

Loyalties Curse

POEM TWENTY-SEVEN

Poem Twenty-Seven

I can't hear what you say if I can see what your doing, your life or my life, somebody's getting ruined, reach for a Goal, what are you pursuing, can't stay for the Funeral, but I'm here for the Viewing, Biting for a Long time, what are you Chewing, really ask yourself, What are you Doing, Tricks under my Sleeve, I got something Brewing, Mouthwatering, I Might catch you Drooling, Everybody Knows, Who you think you Fooling, Small of my Back, is how I snuck the Tool in, Patiently waiting, For the Judge's Ruling, Stayed after Class, For the Teachers Schooling, All out of Gas, Time for Refueling, This ain't for Everybody, only let a Few in, Misunderstood, Legitimate Confusion.

Loyalties Curse

POEM TWENTY-EIGHT

Poem Twenty-Eight

Butter Soft your Biscuit, don't make me Jelly your bread, 5 pounds of Pressure, Now we gotta Spread, New meal at the Dinner table, make Sure Every Body Gets Fed, See no Evil, Hear no Evil, He might be a Fed, Demonstrations make you Sleepy, Here's a Pillow for your Head, Twisted Formations from your Rooftop, Something we all Dread, Some things we never Mention, Make sure it Never gets Said, Numbers on your Memory Block, that's a Price on your Head, Words Hurt the Heart of Strangers, Don't Die for something you Said, They might Stain your shirt, a colorful Red,6 feet Deep, What a Wonderful Bed, Treat your body like a Pencil, and Fill it with Lead, You Came here to Work, and got sent home instead.

Loyalties Curse

POEM TWENTY-NINE

Poem Twenty-Nine

If the Sun don't shine, the Son don't Shine, take care of yours I'll take care of mines, P80 in the Trunk, we all got Nines, never say it again, If you said it a million Times, Ladders for everybody, we all gotta Climb, never carry loose change, nobody dropping Dimes, They use your words against you, we never talk about Crimes hit the Bodeda for a Corona, Poppy got the limes, Take a Sample off two Bricks, don't forget your Lines, a couple of strong soldiers, but they nothing like mines, All the bullets are mental, they Only attract your Mind, make your body Shake, you can feel it in your Spine, we don't leave witnesses, nothing gets left behind, Room full of Monsters, we all the Same Kind, Searching for Peace, But what did you Find, Speeding Through a Red Light, But you get Stopped at The Sign, You had to Hear it again, So You Pressed rewind, You Don't Remember the Day, But I remember the Time, No use in a Barbershop, Ain't nobody getting Lined, Your card has no Value, if it keeps getting Declined. Get your Money Up, Never Tell Nate you in a Bind.

Loyalties Curse

POEM THIRTY

Poem Thirty

You can't trust a thief, that's still a wolf with no teeth; if you lying don't speak, you might need a priest; if you awaken the beast, when you iron, no crease, rapid fire, no cease, you won't rest in piece, what I say, be the least, at the table, we feast, we await your release, top dog, you the chief, get a sense of relief, in shock disbelief, from the south to the east, my arms got to reach, you gotta listen to each, if you wanna teach, make sure the words in your speech, ain't you trying to preach, the chains off the leash, compromised, there's a breech, Can you find your Peace, Make your bed with no sheets, you live in the Streets, just heard some new beats, You Sew what You Reap, My Missions Complete, But first take a Seat.

Loyalties Curse
POEM
THIRTY-ONE

Poem Thirty-One

Didn't know the Beginning, but I can see the End of You, Didn't know the outside, but I can see the inner you, looking for a job, next week I got a interview, Summer time Maddness, what about the Winter View, Bullets never Pop Out, all they do is Enter You, Your Lifestyle so Pitiful, Sick of being Miserable, left you up in Critical, All your Thoughts, Subliminal, On your Knees Praying, asking God for a Better View, A Long Road Is ahead of You, Hoping it Was Me, But this was Only made for You, Looking like a Vegetable, No lie, This can't be True, No Laces, You never Tied your Shoe, one of one, but I was Made for 2, I was never made for You, Many Men, I paid a Few, Hoping that they Stayed with you, Dancing in Dirt, Only Option is to Lay with You, I ain't Afraid of You, What they Call, will Label You, Brought the Chairs, and the Tables too, WiFi and there's Cable too, Can't move, They stabled You, Wrong Game, Why they Played With You, No test But I Graded You, Thank God I made it Through.

Loyalties Curse

POEM THIRTY-TWO

Poem Twenty-Two

What's yours is Mines, you gotta give it, we can't discuss my life, it's too explicit, before a frog can leap, you hear a Ribbit, take 3 steps, and then you pivot, can't answer the question, so you skip it, it's all in the wrist, you gotta whip it, Your life is your own, you gotta live it, to make a new choice, you gotta pick it, these cookies ain't Sweet, you gotta chip it, if the plan don't work, you gotta fix it, Hold on tight, you gotta grip it, Your mouth is Dry, you need some liquid, Find a coupon, and then you clip it, When the Casket gets closed, you gotta Dip it, Move these Packs, You gotta Ship it, The Opportunity is gone, how did you Miss it, Get caught speeding and get a Ticket, To get the Reward, You gotta Risk it, If you Miss Someone, Then you should Visit, To Give it to God, You Gotta Lift it, The Hate in your Heart, Makes you Wicked, It's only the Sky, There is no Limit.

Loyalties Curse

POEM
THIRTY-THREE

Poem Thirty-Three

I crossed the Ocean just to Make Shore, Opportunity doesn't Knock on a Broken Door, Silence my Speech, I can't move my Jaw, Ups, and Downs, I know I didn't See what I Saw, Remove your shoes, before you step on my Floor, Respect is Bare Minimum, I won't ask you for More, Cleaning Out My Closet, that's my only Chore, Sparkling Lights, can you see the Allure, I don't want what you have, my intentions are Pure, so there's really no need for you to be insecure, Work for myself, as a entrepreneur, my ambition is Driven, but I walk to the Store, Love me in a Special Way, Your So Immature, Ready to Face the Demons, that you try to ignore, My Cup is Half empty, continue to Pour, Sleeping with the Enemy, and find out that she Snore, I don't like who you Became, Take me back to Before, My Destination is Out of this World, I Need Space to Explore.

Loyalties Curse

POEM
THIRTY-FOUR

Poem Thirty-Four

How can I be late if I created time, rubbing two nickels together, won't get you a dime, Follow You without Sight, that's just the Blind leading the Blind, communication without words, you don't know the sign, I can only be myself, I'm really a different kind, Brought me a Pair of Boots, for the Roads I have to Climb, Loyalty will make you Stupid, Don't ever cross that Line, Believe in your Heart it will be OK, Everything will be Just Fine, Younger Version of my Better Self, Thats me in my Prime, Never question what others Say, The Truth Will always Allign, Validation for what I think I know, Lord Please give me a Sign, Slow Movements in a Fast race, Your gonna get left Behind, They listen to Your Phone Calls, Never Speak about Crime, Preparation for a Downhill, but what about the Incline, Sacrifice myself, I'll do it for mine, Here we Go Again, Thats Time after Time, Shoot the Club up and I Only get Blamed, Thats me Trying to Shine, Searching for What's not Inside Myself, Some Things weren't Meant to Find.

Loyalties Curse

POEM THIRTY-FIVE

Poem Thirty-five

I Never been to School cause I already got a Skill, Artificial Intelligence; there's no way to keep it real, 1.99, your more than a cheap thrill, stand behind my enemies, and use them as a shield; Never in the House, you can catch me in the Field, if you slip, I'm a slide, I'm on a banana peel, Get a New Deck, If You dont know how to Deal, Say the Right thing, the wrong words might get you killed, Revenge is a Cold Dish, and you gotta keep it Chilled If Nobody Stands Tall, I'm keeping the Seats Filled, Pour out my Cup, for the Ones that were Spilled, Nailed to a Wall or Died being Drilled, Look in a Mirror the Truth will always be Revealed, Your No Longer Sick, You've already been Healed, Signed and Delivered, It's already been Sealed, Create my own Song, I'm letting the Beats Build.

Loyalties Curse
POEM
THIRTY-SIX

Poem Thirty-Six

I will never tell you what I've done, don't care if you believe, walk around with DNA, got his brain on my sleeves, don't care what you do, as long as you achieve, made his momma cry, she dropped to her knees, play with a dirty dog, you gonna catch some Fleas, Father called me a Germ, he think ima disease, Heart Cold as hell, so I don't care if you freeze, Beg for your life, I wanna hear you yelling Please, Live like a Demon, God wouldn't bless you if you sneeze, hang you by your feet, you can catch him in the Trees, I know how to break a lock, I don't need any keys, didn't have the bread, but now I got the cheese, no toothpaste so all you do is squeeze, catch your first body, this fittin to be a breeze, everything is Gucci, got used to wearing Lee's, This Fires getting Hot, we got different Degrees,

Everything Comes Natural, like the Birds and the Bees, Looking for a Alphabet, we Searching for the Ds, Never give me what I want, all you do is Tease, Lies will set you Up, The truth always Frees.

Loyalties Curse

POEM THIRTY-SEVEN

Poem Thirty-Seven

I didn't come here to Speak; make me a Sandwich instead; nothing you can do will stop my daily bread, Protect the Spots you Cherish the Most; that's Arm Leg Head, Responsible for your own life, now go lay in your Bed, Hungry for your own understanding, think about what's being Fed, Distortion of Popularity, you Rather be Famous than Dead, Face still wet from the Tears that were Shed, 4 Pound Memory Loss, don't let that go to your Head, This Disease will Eat you Alive, don't let it Spread, A Artist and a Paint Brush, Will Paint the Town Red, No Conversations with a Pork Chop, Think about the Words being Said, Natural Life for a Bedrock, But you don't Know Fred.

Loyalties Curse

POEM THIRTY-EIGHT

Poem Thirty-Eight

Bible in my pocket, I got God on my side, Devil on my shoulder, I got no place to Hide, Days at a playground, all we did was Slide, New angels in Heaven, now I got a Guide, all out of tears, cause they all dried, death to my emotions, all my feelings Died, Begged you for the Truth, but you only lied, Two Lions in a Cage, soon they will Collide, Drove right pass me, Now you need a Ride, Shot in the Back, now your Stomach Opened Wide, Married to The Game, who's the Father to the Bride, Give you All I Got, Protect and Provide, Didn't Meet his Mark, but I know he Tried, It's Loyalty or It's Death, you gotta Decide, didn't ask a Question, with no words he Replied, Didn't Pay me Back, Your Credit gets Denied.

Loyalties Curse
POEM
THIRTY-NINE

Poem Thirty-Nine

10 Million ways to Die, You got the Option, to Pick and Choose, We all Play a Deadly Game, But how many know the Rules, I'm taking all the Money, But I'm leaving you the Jewels, If you don't wear Socks, never walk a Mile in another Man's Shoes, Beat up, Battered and Broken, now your all Confused, I didn't come here to Fix it, I don't have any Tools, No man is a Island, It's time to take a Cruise, Couldn't Solve the Story, I left you all the Clues, Paperboy outside, Did you get the News, Alarms going off, No time to Press the Snooze, accepted every Win, But I learn more when I Lose, Some of the Nails are Missing, But I got all my Screws, Guilty til Innocent, Watch who you Accuse, Manipulations only Destiny, Watch who you Confuse, Emotional thoughts Without Feeling, The Lady Sings the Blues.

Loyalties Curse
POEM FORTY

Poem Forty

What don't kill you, will make you weaker, turn me up, so you can hear me in your speaker, strength and beauty, your strongest feature, creature of habit, the Student became the Teacher, Promotion of Death, I Am your Seeker, you will never Trace my Steps, call me a Sneaker, Cold hearted Bloodline, I have no Heater, No way to Disguise this lie, I can't make it no Sweeter, Brand New Baby Girl, I can't wait to Meet her, Congregations Perception of my Demise, I am your Preacher, Stolen Legacy from Across the World, What did you Teach Her, Strength to Make You Strong, Can't Recognize the Weak Her.

Loyalties Curse

POEM
FORTY-ONE

Pour Forty-One

I asked myself was I meant to be here, I got the perception of Why, You can't give it all you got, if you not willing to Try, Stand on everything I step on, that means I'm willing to Die, No sympathy when they get me, So don't you even Cry, Can't Boil every Egg, Sometimes they have to Fry, Tell them I don't know Shit, You gotta ask the Other Guy, I only tell my Family the Truth, Still look at the Judge and Lie, What I Did was done For a Reason, No Difference in you and I, now you got a Wet Face, can't find a Dry Eye, Walk away from madness, I had to Say Goodbye, it didn't go the Right way, but still it was a good Try, Recognize my Strength, Some things you can't Deny, I Always tell the Truth, Even when I Lie.

Loyalties Curse

POEM FORTY-TWO

Poem Forty-Two

My Umi Told me to Shine my light bright, so the world can see, the Gift that was given, was not just for me, something you can't deny, so we all can agree, couldn't keep you to myself, we all Have to See, We all have a greater Purpose, What are you supposed to be, If we all pay attention, everything should be for Free, Sick before birth, So there is no Remedy, two subjects that don't matter, there is no Chemistry, it might cost a percentage, just to interest me, Rearrange your Face, brand new Dentistry, Something like a Adult, There's no Kidding Me, You never saw my Face, But you will always Remember Me, I'm Who You Pretend to Be.

Loyalties Curse

POEM
FORTY-THREE

Poem Forty-Three

I didn't know I was Locked Up, til the day they set me Free, had a long look at my surroundings, and said this couldn't be; caught a glimpse of my Reality; this can't be me; your thoughts is your thoughts, we don't have to Agree, Eyes wide shut, some things you never get to see, all out of coffee, so sip on this Tea, in the Jungle what came first, The Dirt or the Tree, it's all downhill, so you better learn to Ski, all by myself, ain't nobody sitting with Me, You have to Pay Attention, so this lesson here for Free, I never said I'm Sorry, that's no Apology, Ungrateful, Give thanks when you Acknowledge me, Stand Tall, Don't ever Promise me, give back to the Economy, No Brakes ain't no Stopping Me,No Vision ain't no watching me, Doors Locked, But I got the Key.

Loyalties Curse

POEM
FORTY-FOUR

Poem Forty-Four

I wasn't a Nigger til you told me I was One, Bastard to the Moon, shine bright like the Sun, Knowledge and wisdom, I had to get me some, Nectar of The God's, Passion Fruit, Red Rum, Surviving for a Piece, Risk your life for a Crumb, Out here acting like you stupid, lose your life for being dumb, I can't feel a thing, my hands getting 2 numb, I can hear your fear, your heart beats like a drum, hand to hand combat, no need for a Gun, All over the Earth, Let them know where you From, Out here enjoying myself, I'm just trying to have some Fun, Carry on Tradition, This a Letter to my Son, Never Apologize, You ain't finished til it's Done.

Loyalties Curse

POEM
FORTY-FIVE

Poem Forty-Five

Umi didn't raise a Coward, Baba raised a Man, Never mind what I Can't, Only do what I Can, Couldn't afford 2 ,So I'm your only fan, Carried you through Life, that's my imprint in the Sand, A,B, or C I always keep a Plan, They only raise you High, So you Die when you Land, Put me on Top, Next to your favorite Brand, Can't Sit Still, I'm ready to take a Stand, I'm starting to Lose Grip, Things are getting out of Hand, Never about what you negotiate, only about what you demand, Things could be all so Simple, But ⁷This ain't Wu Tang Clan, Death in my Arms, I got your life in my hands, One Guitar 2 drums I'm just trying to make a band.one ounce,2 dimes I'm just trying to make a Grand, No Woman can wear my Shoes, or tell me How to be a Man.

Loyalties Curse
POEM
FORTY-SIX

Poem Forty-Six

It's a long way down, from the Bottom; you told me to get him, so I got him, long-range, Back to Back, til we spot him, Top floor, Sky High, had to drop him, Head from his Crown, is how they got him, the smell of spoiled meat, is always Rotten, can't remember much, so it's all forgotten, Closed Door, one key, now we locked in, can't hold me Back, so I dropped in, on my way to work, had to clock in, One Guitar 2 Drums, now we Rocking, No Presents or Gifts in your Stocking, Didn't Swing one Punch, But you Blocking, Massa got you Out here Picking Cotton.

Loyalties Curse

POEM
FORTY-SEVEN

Poem Forty-Seven

Separate yourself, protection from behind the scenes, strength in numbers, no I in Teams, if we all go to sleep, then we apart of the Same Dreams; I drink my coffee dark, there's rules to this Cream, It can all be so simple, but that's just what it seems, Hit, Like, Share, all for the Streams, red or blue pill, apart of the Machines, Left or right side, no in-betweens, you might ride dirty, but still keep it clean, you don't understand, just know what I mean, even if you look, it still wont be seen, move just like a vegetable, keep it a bean, favoritism with colors, do anything for the Green, Going soft is a Habit, You gotta keep yourself Mean.

Loyalties Curse

POEM FORTY-EIGHT

Poem Forty- Eight

Once it hits you, you will feel no Pain, but after it touches you, you will never be the Same; no driver's license, you driving me insane, one to the Heart, two to the Brain, No Romance in The Jungle, This ain't Tarzan and Jane, Dollar Cab, Footwork, or you Take the Train, Special Delivery from Hot Nickles, I came to bring the Pain, Nobody Knows my Distance, I know how far I came, Testify against No Man, I'm the Only One To Blame, Ketchup Blood or Gravy, This kind of Fabric won't Stain, Walk with My Head Held High, Still don't Say my Name, I Only want the Best for You, Even if you don't Wish me the Same.

Loyalties Curse

POEM
FORTY-NINE

Poem Forty-Nine

What I do is 2+2, you know who I'm Doing it For, Dance you around the Earth, I'll take your ass on tour, give you a small piece, that way you Always want More, first step starts your Path, I have a world to Explore, Opportunity only Knocks, you already know who's at the Door, Drop a Ball in a Basket, I'm just trying to Score, Back to Back, Side to Side, Just don't hit the Floor, Never Turn your back on Forgiveness, Something you can't Ignore, Water whipped understanding, Make moves when you Shore,2 bags of Chips and a Honey Bun, you need anything else from the Store.

Loyalties Curse

POEM FIFTY

Poem Fifty

Gunshots, Gunshots, they wouldn't let her pass,8 mile temptation,40 yard dash, no seat belt, head first, soon she's gonna crash, detonated bomb, all she seen was the blast, Now she's a Monster, that's Strength from a Glass, Unrecognized, no memories of the Past, No days in School, She doesn't have any Class, Lifestyle is Dirty, No wash rag to Harass, Dumpster Dive Tragedy, Show love to the Trash, Already Stepped On, anybody can Smash, Picture Perfect Catastrophe, That's life in a Flash, On Top of the World, But how long did it Last.

Loyalties Curse

POEM
FIFTY-ONE

Poem Fifty-One

Always Pay Attention, that's the cost to be the Boss, understand the Value in a Lesson, Every Loss, ain't a Loss, every time you Fall, get right back on the Horse, don't forget who's watching, never take your eyes off Course, stand on everything you Believe in, live life without Remorse, everything comes naturally, you'll never have to Force, Everything comes from you, You are the Main Source, but Never on a Plate, Your not the Main Course, Gave you half my Rib, No time for a Divorce, Black Love is Special, The only Thing I'm willing to Endorse, Life is a Test and I hope I Pass the Course.

Loyalties Curse

POEM
FIFTY-TWO

Poem Fifty-Two

Prostitute in my shirt, I had a trick up my sleeve, bad father figure, all you did was leave, blessed with a Sickness, but you never heard me sneeze, tried to get a Hug, but all you did was Squeeze, Sacrifice to get Some Bread, I need that for My Cheese, Apologize for Nothing, I already said Please, Pray for my Soul, That's Forgiveness on Your Knees, Make this House a Home, I already have the Keys, The Principle of Being Stupid, supplied only By Greed, I never give you what you want, Only what You Need, Come to an understanding, That Means we Both Agreed, Leave your Thoughts inside a Book, Cause I don't know How to Read, Let My People Go, But they've Already been Freed.

Loyalties Curse

POEM
FIFTY-THREE

Poem Fifty-Three

There comes a time in every man's life, when you gotta toss your pack, and run for your life, can't trust a bullet, I do mines with a knife, can't eat the whole Pie ,I only need me a slice, The Past is what you Have Left, The Future Looks right, do whatever for the dollar, nightmares to survive the night, darkness in every direction, I supplied the Light, Can't give up when your Numbers are Down, There's more rounds to this Fight, Standing on top of a Giant, brought me to a new height, can't eat what you have, I just want a bite, Mastered more of my words, became a wrappers delight, Send memories to Heaven, I attach mine to a Kite, make love in the Opposite of Day, That's a long Kiss Goodnight.

Loyalties Curse

POEM
FIFTY-FOUR

Poem Fifty-Four

Beat up, battered, and bruised, this part of the lesson will leave you confused; never walk a mile in another man's shoes, no time to Play, no games without rules, guard them like treasure; these the family jewels, you know if you know, can't leave any clues, method of madness, it's all how you choose, Either side is a Lesson, it's no win or lose, here to toughen skin, you gotta pay your dues, death comes in 3s, life comes in 2s, lack of Dignity, do it for likes, and Views, Stand up like a Man, forced to refuse, Think for yourself, or end up on the News, Back of a Handle, What it's Like getting Used.

Loyalties Curse

POEM FIFTY-FIVE

Poem Fifty-Five

Everybody wants Joy, but you learn more from Pain; the Experience of Sunshine, would be nothing; without Rain, Blood Soaked Concrete, no way to clean that Stain, we all Fall Down, only strongest, by the weakest Chain, something we all Have in Common, I Know, you can feel, my Pain, Honest Conversations in the Shower, the Truth goes down the Drain, Apart of the Last Men Standing, I'm the one to Remain, Still have on the Same Shirt, the one without a Stain, Brotherly Love overcomes our Differences, You see what Happened to Cain, Thoughts get Revealed on a Curb, Exposed the Lessons that Drive you Insane, Loyalty might get you Hurt, Something I could Never Explain.

Loyalties Curse

POEM
FIFTY-SIX

Poem Fifty-Six

I know I'm hard-headed, but I learned everything you taught me, cherished, everything you brought me; God bless the Dead, I need you right now to Hold Me; the Fires that burn, you used them to mold Me, Pain exists in Life, the One thing you Showed Me, How to Make it when your Gone, nobody Told Me, No Comparison, the New and the Old me, Can't be a Shirt, don't let them Fold Me, Consider my Destination, wherever the Road Be, Can't identify the Body, Nobody Knows Me, I didn't Pick this Life, This the One that Chose Me.

Loyalties Curse

POEM
FIFTY-SEVEN

Poem Fifty-Seven

Young, Gifted, and Black, watch what you attract, what you know, others lack, in silence, you Attack, Knick, nack paddy, wack now he on his Back, Small piece of rock, chopped up, this is Crack, Phone Call, Land Line, never Hit my Jack, Can't talk, late for Work, I was on my way to Stack, I know where you are, but tell me where you at, in a Room full of Strangers, you should never, wear a Hat, Four corner silence, can turn a Dog, into a Rat, disrespectful views, like it's coming from a cat, we are not alike, I could never sit where you Sat, You will never find a Pig, that can scratch his own Back.

Loyalties Curse

POEM FIFTY-EIGHT

Poem Fifty-Eight

I can buy the napkin, but whose gonna wipe your Nose, Fingerprints or Blood Stains, never Dirty up your Clothes, Always Stick to one side, never turn your back on what you chose, Can't take you anywhere, the last time you Froze, Make sure you stand Tall, keep you on your Toes, it all comes naturally, If you do what you suppose, It's all about Entertainment, Sit back and Watch the Shows, You will never be able to Take his Light, Cause Even in Darkness He Glows, No Way to Stop his Growth, Cause Even through Concrete, He Rose, Pay Attention to What He Says, The Knowledge that Nobody Knows.

Loyalties Curse

POEM

FIFTY-NINE

Poem-Fifty-Nine

You never have to tell me twice, I don't need to be reminded, left his Memory on the Floor, now he's open minded, looking for a statement, but you can't find it, they Only Respect you, cause you violent, no please don't, then it get Silent,1 day left, before your retirement, Freshen your Breath, without the Trident, go against the Grain, Cause you Defiant, There when i need You, You Reliant, little man, with the heart of a Giant, Only Trust Yourself, Never a new Client, Bad Paper Work, Don't you Sign it, Take Responsibility, Without a Requirement, Broken Wheel, Brand New Alignment, Open you up, like a new Appliance, Cold World, What a Vicious Climate, No Homework, But You got a New Assignment, Pay me First, Or No Consignment, You Didn't get it From me, Thats False Advertisement.

Loyalties Curse

POEM SIXTY

Poem Sixty

It ain't easy being Me, I've provided, what's been provided, it already belongs to me, asking yourself how could this be, I paid the cost to be the Boss, and it wasn't Free, Eating off your plate, turned you into a Delicacy, soft as a flower, treat you Delicately, showed you a picture of yourself, you said that wasn't me, your greatest gift, was a present left under a Tree, Fighting back and Forth, with no referee, put you back together, with no guarantee, Chill with the Gossip, That's just some iced tea, Comfortable with the Smoke, So you gotta Fight me, 6X8 cell why you didn't right me, Just turned your back politely, Tie your Shoes Tightly, Thoughts of Revenge was Nightly, Brand New Taurus, I came here to Site See, Push your Wig back Slightly, Dead on arrival, It might be, Pressing on the Gas, Ignite Me, I came here to Party, Invite me, What's done in the Dark Will be seen Brightly.

Loyalties Curse

POEM
SIXTY-ONE

Poem sixty-one

Close enough to push you away, I won't be there on time, I'll be gone another Day, tired of speaking the Truth, what more can I say, this house is not a home, be careful where you Lay, if you can't control the Can, be careful where you Spray, Gone til November, I'm not here to Stay, Prepare for your Enemies, Watch where you Prey, I know alot of games, but I didn't come here to Play, If you can't Handle the Rain, Your Flight might get a Delay, Loyalty means Everything, Watch who you Betray, a Couple of Doggie Treats, Watch who you Obey, I know the Real You, Watch who you Portray, Half of your Head is Missing, Your thoughts are on Display, If you want to hear it again you gotta press the replay, This Money Looks Familiar, Same Dollar Different Day, Freedom will cost you Nothing, But you still gonna have to Pay.

Loyalties Curse

POEM SIXTY-TWO

Poem Sixty-Two

The World don't stop; if you Leave, Can't hold your breath, you gotta breathe, The Lord will bless you, if you sneeze, gotta give more than you receive; know in your Heart, you can Achieve, Take care of your wants, and all your Needs, Just know you can kill it, if it Bleeds, Don't let nothing Stop you, You can Proceed, Never Bite a Hand, If it Feeds, Buried in Dirt with all your Seeds, Never Trust a Tongue if it Pleads, Captivity is in your Mind, You've already been Freed, Never in the Back, You gotta Lead, Open the Door, You got the Keys, Slow it down, No reason to Speed, Stacking your Bread and all your Cheese, If your Heart hurts, You gotta Grieve, ask yourself do you Believe, The Writings on the Wall, But can you Read.

Loyalties Curse

POEM SIXTY-THREE

Poem Sixty-Three

If I don't get you the first time, I'm gone spin again, the Streets ain't made for losers, so I play to win, never stutter with your steps, this ain't the time to pretend, couple monsters in your circle, but there's none like Him, never deal with alot of people, by my waist I keep my friend, I might be a little flexible, but I'll never Bend, I didn't know you in the beginning, but I'll be there in the End, You Scared of another Body, I'm comfortable in my own Skin,7 pounds will knock your Jaw Loose, Think about your Chin, Don't know why you did it the First Time, But you better not do it again, Your Lifestyle is Written for you, Thats Word to my Pen, Nobody will get the Message, until you Press Send, Make movements with a Strange Look, Thats just My Evil Grin, Doctors can't Recognize the Body, Whose your Next of Kin, Stand Out in Every Crowd, There's no way for me to Blend, Stand on anything Worth Dying for, Who are you willing To Defend.

Loyalties Curse
POEM
SIXTY-FOUR

Poem Sixty-Four

Dear God, my tears have hit the Floor, cried so many times, I don't even care no more, asking for your help, I need you to open a different door, move without reason, don't know what I'm doing it For, comfortable with less, I won't ask you for more, last one to play, I put up the high score, hit the corner for a Plate, I don't know what's in store, All around the World, I'm taking you on Tour, if I can't kill for my own problems, How you start a War, if the beef ain't cooked, how you eating it raw, a smack to your lips, will probably break your Jaw, watch who you talking to, don't go against the Law, my soul ain't perfect, but I keep my spirit Pure, You can feel it in your bones, That's pain to the Core, sick with the gift, and I can't find the cure.

Loyalties Curse

POEM
SIXTY-FIVE

Poem Sixty-Five

Devoted to Scratching The Surface, you left me here with no purpose, things gotta change, just like Curtis, I make 2 Quarters with every Purchase, what's the first thing that you noticed, no cares in this world, makes you hopeless, trying my best, just to stay Focused, believe in yourself, so you know this, anything can Change, without Notice, Flower Bomb your my Lotus, magical vibes, Hocus Pocus, Lions, and Tigers, all are Ferocious, Can't Stand Rats, I can deal with the Roaches, Always Pay Attention to How you approach us, incomplete Beauty, Your the Magnum to my Opus, With no Words is how I Wrote this, If you need Reference then Show this, one false move will leave you Soulless no force or pressure can control This.

Loyalties Curse

POEM SIXTY-SIX

Poem Sixty-Six

If you Disrespect my Brother, you Might get Smacked with a Chair, swim through the Strongest Current, and Show you that I'm there, you got me, I got You, there's More than one, in this Pair, come for him, I come for you, I'll make Them stop and stare, I'm not talking about my momma's child, Thats something we need to make clear, if you go against My Brother, one of us gotta leave here, come through with your People, and this ass whipping is getting shared, I've been Fighting all my life, so understand I'm fully prepared, No Monsters in the Closet, And Nobody is getting Scared, Might Treat you like a Tire, but nobody is getting Spared, Didn't see a Thing, Your Vision is Impaired, I don't know what you thought, But the Strength of Together can't be Compared.

Loyalties Curses

POEM SIXTY-SEVEN

Poem Sixty-Seven

Gunshots Will Follow you, Probably
Hollow You, Go ahead and Do Your Thing,
You Know Poly Vu, I promise you, Life
lessons, Will Guide you through, If it's not
me, It's Probably You, Bad Taste in my
Mouth, From The Witches Brew, I Can
Teach You a Thing or Two, Selfish, I Never
think of You, a Mistake that's probably
True, Without Me, There is No You,
Attached So it's Just Us 2, What am I
Supposed to Do, Nowhere to Go, Meet me
at the Ron-dae-vu, Arm Leg Head, I'm a
Part of You, Excuse Me, Or Pardon You, No
Threat but I Promise You, No Contract will
Sponsor You, Can't Lie, Be Honest too,
Every Swing, You follow through, Morals
and Principles are Honorable, I Honor You,
Bad Decisions Never Tolerable, If you Need
,1 then Borrow 2,Think about Today, and
Tomorrow Too

Loyalties Curses

POEM SIXTY-EIGHT

Poem Sixty-Eight

There's no Father's in the Mother Land, I got your life in my other Hand, if this don't work, you need a Better Plan, Only Ride the Train, if you Think you Can, Don't like who I am, then be a Better Man, too hot In the Kitchen, then get you a Better Fan, Top of the Shelf, there is no Other Brand, 50 twenties, is another Grand, I'm the Crutch, To help my Brother Stand, If you supposed to be here, then the Gun will Jam, Blessed to be here, don't you understand, Quick on your Feet, Do the Running Man, The Summer can't Do, what the Winter Can, Hunting for a Killer, Like the Son of Sam, Powder in Your nose, do you need a Graham, Strangers treat you Better, Than your Family Can, Usual Suspect but you ain't the Man, Clean up the Scene, using Spic and Span, Learning to Trust My Wings, I'll probably never Land, I only Do the Things, that Nobody Can, Lower Levels of Self, Don't You Understand, Smart as a Pig, You a Cunningham, Chasing Your Dreams, but you never Ran

Loyalties Curses

POEM
SIXTY-NINE

Poem Sixty-Nine

I deserve to Get Old, So please don't Shoot, Catch me at the Bottom, That's me at The Root, Attitude of Destruction, Is part of the Suit, unprotected Peace, that's Part of the Fruit, Walk a Mile in my Shoes, Can you Fit my Boot, Greetings to a Soldier, Is Part of the Salute, Never forget Chasing Your Dreams, is part of the Pursuit, Never argue with Fools, no need for a Dispute, The Ugliest Behavior, The Deception of Being Cute, No fresh air, what you touch, you Pollute, didn't hear a Sound, Your volume is on mute, 2 and 2 together, Is something to Compute, Going the Wrong direction, til I find a better route, A plan has no Meaning until you execute, Your Teacher came to Work, There will be no Substitute.

Loyalties Curses

POEM SEVENTY

Poem Seventy

What do I do with all this Pain, No more Sunshine, no more Reign, Brand new shirt, it already got a Stain, alone with a Mirror, no one Left to Blame, I don't know where I'm going, but I know how far I came, tired of Taking the Bus, so I guess I'll take the Train, never use a indicator, I Stay in my own lane, Just called a Uber, He's driving me insane, Just woke up from a Nightmare, I lost half my Brain, thoughts and memories all down the Drain, Walk with a Limp, I might use my Cane, They keep giving out Testers, but I can't find a Vain, Never become Dependent, You might lose your Chain, Things can always be worse, There's no reason to Complain, I've given it all I got, There's nothing left to Gain, Can't call me Bro, if You don't know my Mama Name, You don't know the Rules, and you Playing the Wrong Game, Nothing left to Talk about, What more can I Explain.

Loyalties Curses

POEM SEVENTY-ONE

Poem Seventy-One

There's a Darkness deep inside you, You must set it free, the Same thing that happened to you, already happened to me, Accept the things you can't change, if it's gonna be, than let it Be, Confinement happens in the Mind, A caged bird was meant to be free, roses grow through concrete, Rotten fruit still hangs from a Tree, mixed with honey and lemon, this the Best kind of Tea, Survived a Downhill Battle, I'm still learning how to Ski, My Life, my understanding, we don't always have to agree, Eyes wide Shut, Everything wasn't meant to See, Dog Day afternoon, Stand still or just Flea, My Opportunity doesn't have To Knock, I already gave him a Key, Man in the Mirror, I'm still concentrating on Me,5 Shots 6 Targets, Thats just a Shooting Spree, The Cost of Living is too High, Every day is a New Fee, Associate, Bachelors, and Masters, That's my 3rd Degree, Loyalty will Cost you Nothing, By my side you were meant to Be, No Worries about anything, I was meant to be Carefree, Make my own Merchandise, Thats just a Product of Me.

Loyalties Curses

POEM
SEVENTY-TWO

Poem Seventy-Two

It Hurts to Kill someone you Love, Sent to a Better Place, The Skies Up above, emotional detachment, I really need a Hug, Chopped in 30 Pieces, Wrapped in a Rug, Tried to tell you the Truth, but all you did was Shrug, Heat Burns your Skin, from a Brand New Slug, Lord please Forgive Me, You can't Be The Judge, Flying Too high, no use for a Drug, Supply you with The Future, you might need a Plug, This means War, so I gave you a Tug, Mask with No Prints, I'm Using OJays Glove, Clean up the Scene, I Gave it a Scrub, Back to Back Side to Side, We Dance in the Club, Only Brought 2 Drinks, It cost me a Dub, It came with a Receipt, pass me my Stub, New Grip on a 38, pass me my Snub, Might wash you down, and Leave you in the Tub, The Teacher ain't here, you Might need a Sub, If I don't Eat, You don't Eat, Pass me My Grub, Your Heart Skips a Beat, when you do it out of Love.

Loyalties Curses

POEM SEVENTY-THREE

Poem Seventy-Three

I Sleep with my sneakers on, so I can chase my Dreams, you do anything for the Likes, you out here Chasing Streams, cant regret my past life, involved with triple beams, cash rules everything around me, i did it all for the cream, Bullets make your heat rise, I can see the Steam, No matter what it looks like, things aint always what it seems, We win together, We lose together, There's no changing Teams, 40x32 you can't Fit in these Genes, No More Excuses, Get it done by Any Means,9-6:30 I'm out here with the Fiends, Deal with anything that comes to You, Stand on Everything that it Brings, Emotional Attachments, I'm out here pulling Strings, No Squares in the Circle, We all got Championship Rings, No cares for What I've lost, there only Material Things, Royal with no Compromise, Kings come from Queens, I don't have to Explain much, if you already know what it Means, Pay attention to the Bird that Flies, But watch the Bird that Sings

Loyalties Curses
POEM SEVENTY-FOUR

Poem Seventy-Four

I hope you spare mines, meet you on any corner and compare 9s, you crossing rare lines, nothing is balanced, this ain't the fair kind, No vision but you leading the Blind, a few minutes, this is short time, Crime only leads to more Crime, Scared of the box so you dropped a Dime, Transformer you Optimus Prime, Raised in the Dark but still I Shine, rub two rocks together, I'm on my Grind, Looked under my Bed, what did you Find, you won't be able to sit without your Spine, can't get it back, this a waste of time, 2 Faggits you came from Behind, Baby Steps, this a Nursery Rhyme, To the Top I have to Climb, Please lord show me a Sign, if it's All Right, Then Everything is Fine, Tell you the Truth, I won't be Kind,100 for Your Head, Thats Money on your Mind, Put you in a Box that's made from Pine, Part the Sea turn water into Wine, Built Different, This a part of my Design,1 second this the Last Time.

Loyalties Curses

POEM
SEVENTY-FIVE

Poem Seventy-Five

I came to you Hurting, and you took away the Pain, I came to you With Dirty Clothes, and you Cleaned Every Stain, So Close to Fire, but I Never felt the Flames, Told me to Forget about What I Had, And only Deal with What Remains, Gave me the Want to Give up Jewelry, My Body is No longer in Chains, Supplied Me with the Antidote, No more Poison in My Veins, Had to Listen to Myself, No More Voices in My Brains, Time to Take Flight, My Journey is on the Planes, With or Without, I have no Reason to Complain, I Can only say Thank You, I never have to Explain, Surrounded by Guilt, I have no One I can Blame, You Loved me from Dirt, But you Never Knew My Name, You are Not Special, I Treat All my Children the Same.

This Book is Dedicated to the Life of Michelle K. Joseph. May you Rest in Peace.

Mommy, I Miss You.

FREE CHUBBS

I won't let anybody forget you.

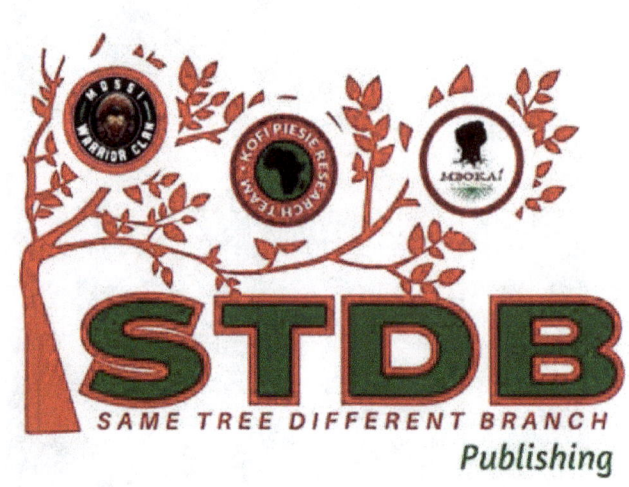

LOYALTIES CURSE

POETRY BOOK VOL 2

COMING SOON

www.ingramcontent.com/pod-product-compliance
Lightning Source LLC
Chambersburg PA
CBHW071211160426
43196CB00011B/2253